Finding Financial Independence

Life With The Stevens Series

Book I

ERROL ANTHONY STEVENS

FINDING FINANCIAL INDEPENDENCE. Copyright © 2020. Errol Anthony Stevens.

All rights reserved. Printed in the United States of America. No part of this book may be used or reproduced in any manner whatsoever without written permission, except in the case of brief quotations embodied in critical articles or reviews.

www.hcpbookpublishing.com

Book and Cover design by HCP Book Publishers

ISBN: 9798664020588

First Edition: 2020

I want to dedicate this book to my parents, Errol Anthony Stevens Snr. and Arlene Stevens.

Also, to my grandparents, wife; Ekaterina Nikiforova Stevens, and my two lovely boys; Lionel and Daniel Stevens.

Special Dedication to My Patreons

This book would not have been possible without the support of my loyal Patreons. I wanted to thank you in the best way possible. May you share this book with your children and grandchildren so they can know we contributed to each other's journey in a big way.

Below are the names of some of my Patreons at the writing of this book:

    Jacqueline Smith
    Jelisa Cameron - Humphrey
    Devena Codner
    William Alphanso Richards
    Sasha Williams
    Seamoune & Ainsworth Maddan
    Robert Headley
    Dwain Brown
    Winston Davis
    Javian Thomas
    Kemesha Alexander

Special thanks to all my other Patreons, whose names are not listed here. I really appreciate you guys.

Acknowledgment

I take this opportunity to thank C. Orville McLeish, CEO of HCP Book Publishing, for accepting to hold my hand through the writing and publishing of this book. He encouraged me and gave me a chance to put in a book, something that was only a thought. With your help, C. Orville McLeish, this book has become a reality; and I know this is only the beginning.

I thank my parents, grandparents, aunt and uncles who all raised me. I was lucky and blessed to have so many God-fearing people in my young life that made me the man I am today.

Special thanks to my beloved wife, Ekaterina Nikiforova Stevens. I love you with all my heart. Thank you for believing in me. My story is what it is because of you. You saw something in me that very few people saw.

To my sons, Lionel and Daniel, you are my driving force and because of you, I have become an ambitious man. You make me want to conquer the world and everything in it; and pass it on to you, so that you may prosper in health, wealth and wisdom.

Table of Contents

Special Dedication to My Patreons v
Acknowledgment vii
Introduction 13
Financial Independence 13
Chapter 1: Adversity Provokes Growth 15
Chapter 2: Between a Rock and a Hard Place 19
Chapter 3: Home Sweet Home 21
Chapter 4: The Wealthy Own 23
Chapter 5: Ownership Attracts More Wealth 31
Chapter 6: Wealth With a Purpose 37
Chapter 7: The Influence of Environment 41
Chapter 8: Give Something to Get Something 45
Chapter 9: The Joys of Passive Income 49
Chapter 10: Riding With Opportunity 53
Chapter 11: Giving Back to My Roots 55
Chapter 12: Spin Many Wheels 59
Chapter 13: Diamonds in the Dirt 63
Chapter 14: Riches Are For Positive Minds 67
Final Word 71

Financial independence is attained by the kind of mind that creates a glorious ending out of murky beginnings

Introduction
Financial Independence

My dad always said, he doesn't want to experience his milk and honey in heaven; rather, he wants it here on Earth. If you read my first book, "To Hell and Back," then you would understand where my father was coming from. I am a 34-year-old retired football player, who grew up in Jamaica. I experienced intensely difficult times growing up in Jamaica, and during my career around the world. I experienced the nasty sting and venom of racism, as I struggled to make my football dream a reality. Despite all the odds I faced since childhood, I am now a happily married man with two children; living off my family investments.

I wrote this book based on my own real life experiences, to educate and inspire younger Jamaicans about how important it is to build wealth, to own assets rather than liabilities, to build a strong and healthy family environment, and most importantly, to build one's faith in Jesus Christ. If I am doing it, so can you!

This book is a blueprint to your financial freedom and, consequently, your freedom for a full life. I pray that God may use this book to equip you with His wisdom and to give you courage to fight for your financial freedom and growth.

Chapter 1
Adversity Provokes Growth

It was in 2018 when I filed a legal FIFA case against my Vietnamese club because of lack of payment. During this time, I was ordered to stop all football activities. I was not allowed to play until FIFA issued a clearance for me to do so. By then I was living with my wife and kids in Vietnam. My eldest son, Lionel, was already more than two years into school in Vietnam, and he was speaking Vietnamese. Swaggy (my wife's pet name) the love of my life, and I, were focused on making all the sacrifices needed to make sure that we would never be short of providing for our sons, Lionel and Daniel. Both our boys were born in Vietnam. To this day, Vietnam gave us everything, even though we started our Journey in Thailand in 2014. Swaggy and I actually met on social media, and we were ashamed to tell anybody of this social media tale for fear of stigma. We were so shy about our social media romance tale that we didn't mention it in our book "To Hell and Back." I realise now that there is nothing to be ashamed of, and that any path which would have led me to my beloved Swaggy was worth treading.

Swaggy gave up her whole life in Russia to follow her heart. She was in her first year in university when she jumped on a plane and flew for hours to a guy she met on vk.com; a Russian site like Facebook. Her friends thought she was crazy to do this for a black man she had never met physically. They thought I would get her pregnant then abandon her in a foreign country. However, Swaggy saw something in me that I didn't even see in myself. I remember waiting at the airport in Bangkok to pick Swaggy up. Her flight had been delayed; I felt as though my heart was skipping beats at a time during the difficult wait. Even though we couldn't get enough of each other over the phone, meeting each other in person would be the test of all times.

When Swaggy walked towards me for the first time, I was thrilled to see her, yet I felt shy at the same time. We cuddled and talked in the taxi, all the way to where I was staying in Saraburi, a small city two hours outside of Bangkok. I lived in a small flat with no kitchen, slept on an Asian mat and rode a simple bike; that was what Swaggy came to. She did not come to a rich football player; she came to someone fighting to find his way in life; all these did not change how she felt about me. We spent every moment together when I was not training or playing. The plan was that Swaggy would visit me for two weeks, then go back home. However, after the two weeks, Swaggy cried and said she did not want to leave me. I begged her to the point of frustration to go home because I did not have the financial capability to take care of her. I told her, "Swaggy, if I lose my job as a football player, I wouldn't be able to take care of you. I cannot afford tickets for us both to Jamaica and I don't even have a home in Jamaica for myself." I was still living with my mother and sister back home in Jamaica. I loved Swaggy, but I was also fearful and realistic. Why would I want to bring her into my struggle? She had a family and a university education to go back to. However, Swaggy was determined to stay by my side. She said she would work at Burger King if it meant that she gets to stay with me. I gave up! I realised that all my efforts to convince her to go back to her stable life were futile.

This was my financial turning point. I started to put in extra hours to make sure I would be the best football player I could be; I had something to motivate me. I realised what a treasure Swaggy was and had to do all I could, the only way I knew how, to keep her. I had to build a life where we would both be happy. At that time, being rich was not even my priority; having a home and food on the table were my priority. It was my first full season in Thailand when Swaggy came, and I took my Division One team to the premier league in Thailand for the first time in the club's history. I guess the love of my life was my good luck charm. However, we had a bigger problem. Swaggy came to Thailand in January 2014 and

Finding Financial Independence

had stayed in Thailand until October. She had overstayed by nine months. We were not yet married, which meant I could not arrange for her stay in the country under my name. She risked being banned from returning to the country for one year. If the police caught her, she would have been deported.

During this season, a Vietnamese club came to scout for me. They were so impressed that they actually signed me from my club in Thailand. It was perfect timing; even though I had one more year on my contract with my Thai club. I explained to my president that my girlfriend was not able to stay in the country and I would not stay without her. The negotiation between Saraburi FC and Hai Phong FC for my transfer therefore begun. We were saved from our situation. We packed all our bags and left Thailand with just one game to go in the season. I did not even stay to celebrate our team's great season.

Chapter 2
Between a Rock and a Hard Place

Let me take you back to 2018. I was jobless because football was my only source of income. I did not have any reason to stay in Vietnam anymore, so we started to plan what to do next while we waited for FIFA to decide on the case. We did not know our fate because Swaggy was from Russia and I from Jamaica. We eventually decided that Jamaica would be the better option. I had my experience with racism, and it scarred me for life; being chased by three males with ill intention in Moscow, while leaving a supermarket in 2009. We could not picture our boys going through that, so Jamaica it was.

Jamaica was not perfect. For many years, I had fears of returning home. I watched the news and saw how residents returning home from the diaspora where being killed. Even regular Jamaicans in general brought real fear into my heart. Vietnam was peaceful; we could leave our doors open and that was what I wanted for my boys. I had been in Vietnam for four years and I had my resident card. If I spent one more year in Vietnam, I would be qualified to be a citizen. I could have lived in Vietnam but, as a black man, there was something uncomfortable about being in another country other than my own. I just could not see myself living in Vietnam, even though I owed everything to it. We were between a rock and a hard place. We moved back to Jamaica in September 2018.

Chapter 3

Home Sweet Home

When we got to Jamaica, I told Swaggy we would rent first to see if she would like the country. We rented a place in Caribbean Estate, Portmore, for three months. It was my first time in that community, and I felt as if we had moved to Florida. The community was nice and peaceful, and we felt so comfortable moving around in Jamaica, because we did not have people always staring at us for being black and white, like it was in Asia. The boys fit in perfectly. Lionel started school at Small Treasures, and he loved it. In Vietnam, he did not have friends in school, but in Jamaica, he was instantly loved. I could tell he was always happy to go to school, and that was when Swaggy and I decided that we would buy our first home in Jamaica.

We purchased our new home in December 2018 at Phoenix Park Village. It was our proudest moment. I did not tell Swaggy, but I cried the first few nights when we moved in. I used to get up and go in the kitchen and I would always sing, "He Saw The Best In Me." To this day, every time I hear that song, I cry.

I was born and raised in Portmore Lane in my early years. We then moved to Greater Portmore and I shuffled between my mom at Greater Portmore and my dad at Seaview Gardens. To now settle my family in a gated community and to let my boys have their own room was really a proud moment for me; it was better than any award I got while playing football.

I started to feel what it really meant to build wealth. I found a purpose other than living for me; I was now feeling what it felt to give something to my kids, and it made me want more. Life is short and we can't take anything with us, but we can leave it for our kids as generational wealth. The Word of God says in Proverbs 13:22, "**A good *man* leaves an inheritance to his children's children...**" (ESV). When I leave this earth, I hope to leave my children with more than what my parents left me; and my parents gave me a lot; they gave me strong principles and that has been my foundation.

Chapter 4
The Wealthy Own

By simple definition, an asset is that which brings you profit, while a liability is that which costs you, in terms of money, time and energy.

We now had a place to call home, but we still did not have any income. In reality, we just created more expenses for ourselves. We now had electricity and water bills, and property taxes to be paid. What I learnt from this was that our home that we live in was our liability. People will define their homes as their asset, but for us, our house was still a liability.

We embarked on finding a true asset. We wanted something that created passive income; something that would not need us to be there physically to tend to it all the time. We wanted to make our money work for us, instead of us working for our money. We had many ideas, such as: starting a taxi company, a wholesale, etc. I remember calling my dad, who had been an accountant for over twenty-five years. He was my first employer. He had a few wholesale companies that he did accounts for. When I called him, he said to me, "Junior! If you open a wholesale, you will have to be the first one to report to work and the last one to leave." He told me a story of how one of his clients used to have to check the garbage when the workers took them out, because they used to throw the store's goods inside the trash bags and pretend it was garbage, only to come back after the wholesale store was closed at night or early morning to pick them up. Opening a wholesale store was therefore a no for me. I hated the thought of a 9-5 or a job that would demand a significant amount of my time, that would take me away from my boys and my wife; being the son of a boss groomed me into this sentiment. I saw how hard my father worked; and while he lives a great life without money worries, he gave up a lot of family time. Even though we, as his kids, understood that he was just making sure we had all that we needed, we missed out on making precious memories together. I am thirty-four years old at the writing of this book, and I still wish I had more time with him. My dad works seven days a week and would sometimes be at work from 6:30am up to 10pm. As the boss, he has to make sure the work is done for the clients; and the more clients he took on, the more work he had. The hours in a day are not added to fit that type of work. He therefore did not have enough time to spend with us.

My dad may have had thoughts of me taking over his company one day, but I think it would have been a nightmare for me. I wanted to have a good life like my dad, but I wanted to let the money work instead of me. I started to read books and learn about how the rich got wealthy, or, to say it more accurately, how the rich created wealth. What surprised me was that most of them did it through real estate. At that moment in time, I had a plan to buy a house and divide it into different sections to rent out. I was focused on getting a home in Greater Portmore as it would be cheaper than buying an apartment in Kingston. Furthermore, most Greater Portmore houses do not carry high maintenance fees like apartments in Kingston. Actually, for regular Greater Portmore houses, there was no maintenance fees paid outside of what you would spend to maintain your property. When I did my research, I realized that to buy a two-storey house in Greater Portmore would cost me the same amount of money as buying a house in the gated community. This puzzled me as a young man who was just getting into real estate. I thought to myself, "Why not buy another house where I lived?" However, I also thought that if the community started to lose value or get "run down", as Jamaicans would say, I would not want both my homes in the same area. I also figured that if I bought another home in the same community and rented it to one family, the rent could not cover all my expenses. I would only receive rent of 75,000 JMD per month. The return on investment would be too small. I was learning about bonds at the time and I went to JMMB to find out about a bond; it was around 6% per annum, which did not sound bad, but it could not cover the needs of my family of four. I liked the idea of owning assets, so I went back to the drawing board.

While I was in Vietnam, I was thinking about getting a house in Florida. My brothers, who had migrated to the USA, were living there. I thought to myself, "Why not buy one close by and rent it out?" The return on investment seemed to match my family budget; we could have easily rented for 1,400USD a month, and that was enough to meet all our expenses. However, what stopped me from buying the house was that it would be hard for me to manage the home from Jamaica, and the property taxes in America were too high for my liking; there were a lot of taxes that came with owning a home in America. Homeowners association fees where pretty high as well. I knew a home was going to be my best investment, but I was not in a rush to purchase just any house or apartment; I wanted the right one. In pursuit of this, I met a lady by the name of R. Stevenson. She was a realtor I was working with to find homes in Jamaica. During a conversation with her, she asked me a very good question. She knew I wanted a home, but she asked what was my reason for wanting the home. She asked this because she noted that I already had a home where I lived. I told her that I needed something to generate passive income; income from rental properties which did not need me to be actively involved in generating the money. I needed a cash flowing property. I told her of my idea to find a property in Greater Portmore, divide it up into four units, then rent out each unit for 25,000JMD. This was the trend amongst Jamaican landlords. I would end up with 100,000JMD every month. However, I realised after much thought, that dealing with tenants can be a stressful mess. Mrs. Stevenson told me, "Why not buy a beach front apartment, then convert it to an Airbnb? You will then earn in USD."

I was thrilled to hear such a statement. I had never thought of a beach front apartment and I did not even know those could be sold to individuals. Even though I now own an apartment at Fisherman's Point, because of my background, I would have thought those properties were run by some big company and I had no clue they could be individually owned. I also did not think it was possible to earn in USD while in Jamaica; not many businesses in Jamaica can achieve that. I was open to her idea and super excited at the time. She sent me the profiles of a few properties and asked me to look over them. When I saw what I liked, we went and viewed them. I also did my research about Airbnb. I had heard the term but had no idea what it was. I learnt that Airbnb is used by tourists for more affordable accommodations; much cheaper than the hotels. I also learnt that any ordinary home can be turned into an Airbnb. I went further to research about the existing Airbnb in Jamaica and found a guy by the name of Havanah. He was in charge of the Airbnb association of Jamaica. I sought for his phone number and gave him a call. When I told him who I was, he was pretty excited to hear from me; I was a well-known professional football player. We ran over ideas and he showed me properties in Kingston, which he owned and was working on. He also showed me others in Ocho Rios, which he had on his portfolio. He managed properties for other owners as well. In addition, he leased properties from owners and used them as Airbnb; and it was working. Havanah had properties that charged 100USD a night, that were almost always fully booked. When I did my calculations, I was stunned to know that people were earning 2-3,000USD a month from Airbnb in Jamaica. I was excited.

I told Havanah about Mrs. Stevenson's idea and we noticed that they both had a similar idea. However, Havanah's idea was somewhat different; he thought, instead of me buying just one property, I could use the same deposit money to lease multiple properties like he was doing, and then put them all on Airbnb. When we did our calculation, it turned out that I could lease around ten properties. However, like I said before, I am a reserved person who does not rush into investing. I like thinking through the investment before I start. I asked

Havanah questions like, "What if we couldn't get the places booked and we had to come up with the owners rent just the same?" I realised that leasing did not fit my plan of ownership at that time. I had this firm belief, "The wealthy own!" I was therefore more interested in owning property instead of leasing, even if I would conquer slowly a home at a time. I was not focused on quick money; to me, it was better to own a few businesses but of high quality. This was one of my principles. I wanted to own something that I can leave for my kids as an inheritance.

Chapter 5
Ownership Attracts More Wealth

Havanah tried for days to convince me to lease. We set out on sail to Ocho Rios to look at two properties. Havanah used the services of a realtor by the name of Rohan Scott, who became a good friend of mine to this day. I had never met Havanah personally; we always spoke on the phone and this was the first time we met. He brought Rohan along and he set up the viewing for two properties: one at Fisherman's Point and the other at Sandcastle. We took the new highway from St. Catherine to Ocho Rios; it was my first time on the highway. In 2013, when I left for Thailand, the only way to get to Ocho Rios was by going over flat bridge. Therefore, seeing the highway and how fast we got to Ocho Rios; that was a marvel. The mountains and the beauty of Jamaica gave me a sense of pride. We got to Ocho Rios; it was my first visit to Ocho Rios as an adult. Before that, I had only been to Ocho Rios on school trips, to Dolphin Cave, Dunns River and the Jerk Centre. I had never been to the town of Ocho Rios, let alone Fisherman's Point or Sandcastle. Therefore, I was marvelled upon arriving at Fisherman's Point and getting to the gate where we could see Island Village to the left. There were a lot of tourists. I was in awe! We got inside the premises we came to view, and I was pleasantly shocked. I turned to Rohan and asked him, "Isn't this a resort? Isn't it privately owned by one owner?"

"No Bro." He answered in his American accent. Rohan lived in the States and came back to Jamaica. He got the key and while walking to the apartment, I saw a swimming pool and I was in awe of this place. I might sound crazy, but I was from Portmore Lane and Seaview Gardens. The property we were viewing was way out of my league and comfort zone, but I held it together. When we arrived in the room, we found an English lady staying there; a tourist. Even though the room should have been empty, she was there; she was given the room by a devious staff who was doing it as a hustle under the owner's nose. I brought my wife and kids along. My wife was pretty excited too. Rohan asked us to wait outside while he called the owner. He then spoke to the tourist who rented the apartment to let us in. She was a nice white English lady; she allowed us in. Me being my friendly self, I engaged the lady in a casual conversation. I wanted to see her point of view as a tourist. She told me she loved the location, the beach, everything. She told me she came to this same place every year. I shared with her that my wife and I planned to buy the apartment. She was happy for us. I also asked as politely as I could, how much she was paying per night. She told me that she got a special rate of £89 pounds. I quickly took out my phone and multiplied it by twenty-five nights and my mouth was left opened in shock and excitement. I composed myself quickly. I did not know Rohan so well at the time. I told Swaggy before we left the car, "No matter how much you love the place, find all the faults and never look interested; we need to get it at a good price." We giggled mischievously, then we went on to carry out our plan.

My dear wife has an eye for detail. Swaggy found every fault in the place. Not even one fault escaped her eye, and she was vocal about it. Honestly speaking, the main fault was the miss-matching tiles on the floor, and the room looked like 1986, the year the place was built. When we came out of the apartment, Rohan and Havanah asked what we thought. We told them we wanted to buy it. They were surprised. "What about Sandcastle?" They asked, "Don't you want to see it?" I declined, but Havanah was still into the idea of leasing multiple properties for Airbnb business. He convinced us to just go have a look.

Sandcastle was just down the block. We drove back down the street and went in. While we were parking, I noticed they had a tennis court. I was impressed for a moment. However, when we got around to the swimming pool area, we found it being renovated. That was a turn off for me. It looked like it was going to be that way for months. Havanah then took me to the back and I saw what I could not believe: Ocho Rios Bay beach. Even when we went to Fisherman's Point, I had no idea there was a beach around the back. This all sounds so funny to me now, but I was lost for words. Swaggy was still in the car with the kids so she did not see the beach at all. While I was still mesmerized, Havanah said, "Yes, if you own one of these apartments, you will have free access to the beach. It's private." I still cannot find the words to explain how I really felt at that moment. I imagined being a tourist in my own country; I was seeing the beauty and potential of Jamaica right before my eyes, that most Jamaican youth never get to see or enjoy.

We went up to the apartment in Sandcastle and it was a beautiful room. I found it even more beautiful than the room at Fisherman's point. It was a bigger room; two bedrooms; and it was selling for the same price as the one bedroom at Fisherman's Point. I was impressed. It was a two-floor apartment and it even had a rooftop and a beautiful view of the ocean. I was starting to think twice about the apartment I wanted to buy, but while walking through, I noticed the roof had a lot of water marks; it seemed like it was a leaking roof. That was the biggest turn off. When we went back to the car, I described to

Swaggy what I saw. Just like me, Swaggy had already made up her mind that it was going to be Fisherman's Point. We told Rohan of our plans and that we did not share the same idea as Havanah about leasing. We wanted to own the apartment. I wanted to give my kids something they could own for life. I had this feeling that the area would grow into something beautiful; and that to own it would be the best move. Rohan shared my values; he preferred building and owning real estate over leasing. Rohan is a smart man. I mean, he is like a walking library. He knows his history, he knows everybody's history, he understands life and he can put things in words in a way that perplexes me. I have always been street smart, but not so much book smart or words smart. God has gifted me with common sense, and it has never failed me yet. I am also blessed with great intuition; if I follow my heart, I never go wrong. Every time I follow my gut feeling, I make the right decision, but every time I ignore it, it costs me.

We started the process to buy the property. I got a lawyer and Rohan hooked us up with the owner and their lawyer. The purchasing process was set in motion and by March 2019, I was the new owner of the apartment at Fisherman's point. Owning this apartment was my first step into being wealthy, because when everyone else is renting, the wealthy own. I thank God.

Chapter 6
Wealth With a Purpose

Before the apartment was officially handed over to us, we went to see it one more time. We wanted to evaluate it and plan on what we would need to do to get it looking modern. We asked Rohan and my lawyer if they could request the seller to allow us to view it. She was a Jamaican Lady who moved to Liverpool, England, after getting married to a white English man. Yes, it is very important for me to describe her in detail, because the story I will tell you next is one that changed my life, along with many good stories. She agreed and gave us a date. We did not miss the opportunity, the place was still being rented while we bought it; it was therefore important to use the time and window she gave us. We set out to Ocho Rios; this time with just Swaggy, the kids and my sister Jody; we knew our way there this time.

When we arrived, to our surprise, there was another lady in the room. This time, it was not a tourist; it was the owner herself. She was an elderly lady; old enough to be my grandmother. She greeted us with love and a warm smile. I introduced my wife, sister and kids to her. She called a young man from the room as we were sitting in the living room and introduced him as her son. He resembled my boys, but he was older than me. While Swaggy and my sister looked around, planning the decorations and future renovations, the lady said to me, "Do you know why I choose to sell this apartment to you?"

I was surprised; I was thinking to myself, "I'm the one buying it from you." I mistakenly thought I was the one who had the upper hand in the choice to buy it. "Yes, to you!" she continued.

I said, "No ma'am."

She then said, "You are black and young; and out of all the buyers, you are the only black one. Out of all the people I know who own apartments here, you're one of the few Jamaicans. Most owners live overseas and are not Jamaican; therefore, the money being made here doesn't go back into Jamaica. It does not go to the economy or to the people of Jamaica. For this reason, I wanted to make sure I sold it to a Jamaican!" Those words, my friend, along with all the racism I had been through, along with everything else that was happening in my life; those words gave me a sense of purpose. I also felt good that someone was looking out for me in business, like a mother would for her son. That lady changed my thinking and therefore my life, without even knowing. From that moment on, I became more Jamaican than I ever was. I wanted to tell every Jamaican what that lady had told me; I wanted to see more Jamaicans owning a piece of Jamaica.

Even as I write this book, I have a YouTube channel called, "Life with the Stevens " and a second one, "The Errol Stevens Show" where I preach to Jamaicans about building Jamaica; about loving and investing in Jamaica; because there is no place like Jamaica. I started a patreon account where I can communicate with my subscribers on YouTube, and I have been able to help one patron so far to buy and own an apartment at Fisherman's Point. This person is now one step closer to being financially independent, and it all started from when that elderly lady told me those words of wisdom. If that was not Jesus at work, then I don't know who. I am set to make sure that every Jamaican knows what they are sitting on; Jamaica is paradise. We all cannot sit here and wait for life to happen. We may have to go to other countries to find opportunities that give us the empowerment we need for wealth, but I urge you, once you get enough to even start small, come back and invest in Jamaica. Invest in your country and your people, because there is no place where you can live life to the fullest like home. Let us build Jamaica to an extent where people around the world come to look for opportunities here. Let us leave a great inheritance for our children.

I myself had to leave to find greener pastures on the other side of the world because of lack of opportunities, but the best thing I ever did was to return home. There is a lot of negativity about Jamaica, some of which is true. But the good outweighs the bad, and we can use the good to turn the bad into good; we have the power to do so. Think about it this way, if you have a child and that child is behaving badly, do you abandon the child? Do you kick that child out into the streets and think he will get better on his own? No! You must show love to that child; you must motivate that child; you must give that child hope and dreams; and this is what we need to do for Jamaica. We don't need the Prime Minister to accomplish this; we need every Jamaican to put his brother and sister first; and I am not talking your brother from your mother, I am talking about your neighbours and those in need around you; I am talking about me and you. My biggest pleasure now is helping people to find what I have found. I can take care of my family and I want that for all Jamaicans. It is my desire to see each Jamaican transform from being the man with the gun to being the man with the Bible. We can create a better Jamaica. We need to educate the youth on life; we need to change the poverty culture. We can transform Jamaica into a wealthy nation.

Chapter 7
The Influence of Environment

I lived in Vietnam for roughly 5-6 years. When I first arrived in Vietnam, I was generally a very angry young man. However, my anger was tamed because the environment was different. You see, in Jamaica you must be a strong fighter in order to not be preyed upon by your brothers and sisters. Vietnam, on the other hand, is a communist society because of the war. Vietnamese people are like one big family. I was once told by one of my African teammates, "No matter what you do, never start a fight in Vietnam as a foreigner in the streets, because all Vietnamese will choose the Vietnamese man or woman's side, even if he or she is wrong." I laughed.

I remember after being in Vietnam a couple of years, I had to get around via motorbike. I noticed something; if someone knocked another person off a bike, they would never stop to pick them up, especially in a busy area. It would be someone from behind on another bike who would come quickly to help someone they did not know. Now, in my Jamaican mind, I was thinking, "If that would happen to me, that would be a straight fight!" I later learnt why they did things this way. After being in Vietnam for years and being able to speak Vietnamese enough, an old Vietnamese man explained to me that it was because they do not want people fighting; that is why they ask the person who caused the accident to go. It is tradition; and the people behind will not hesitate to pick up the fallen person. It is only if the person who falls is badly injured that the person who did it must stop. In a country of 100 million people, with 90% of them using motorbikes as their mode of transportation, you can imagine how often people fall from bikes. I have fallen a lot myself.

My anger level while in Jamaica was really high, but the longer I stayed in Asia, the more it toned down. I could tell I was changing and, me being me, I was trying to figure out why. Was it the music?

Jamaica is a country that is known for music; ask anyone and everyone around the world which musician is the greatest of all time; they will tell you, Bob Marley. I grew up hearing a lot of dancehall music as a child. I must say it had an effect on my subconscious thinking, introducing a little bit of chaos. It spoke mostly of sexual content and killing one another. I remember training one day and I got so hot tempered because a teammate had made a bad tackle. An old Vietnamese man who respected me very much as a player later told me he did not like my hot temper. He noticed, over a period of time, that I got angry easily. He said to me in Vietnamese, "There's a saying that states, 'Only weak people get angry', and that's why Vietnamese are so calm. A person who is really strong can control his or her anger. So, are you strong or weak?"

I replied, "Strong." This conversation changed my life. I must say that, as a Jamaican man, I realized that my home raised me to think that strength is shown through anger and fighting, but I learnt that this was really a weakness; I was far from being strong. Since that day, I can say I am not the same person I was before.

Changing culture can have an immense impact on a society. I sometimes wish I could get all my Jamaican brothers and sisters to see things the way I do. I think it would go a long way in helping to reduce the crime in our country.

I know you may not be able to choose the environment you were born and raised in, but you can choose the people you surround yourself with and what you give your attention to. Choose to hang out with people who are strong in your weak areas. Choose to surround yourself with people who have achieved what you would like to achieve. Choose what you listen to. As much as possible, listen to things that provoke positive thoughts in your mind. These will influence the direction of your thoughts and actions and, therefore, your level of achievement.

Chapter 8
Give Something to Get Something

Back to the apartment, it puzzled me why a lady would sell a property that was doing so well and was in such a great location. When I asked her about it, she told me she was having problems with the property manager. Since she was living abroad, she was not able to be hands on with it herself. She was not able to monitor what was going on in her apartment in Jamaica, from England. She said every time she came to the apartment, she found it mismanaged and in bad condition. That is why she decided to part ways with it to avoid further loss. This information did not deter me from purchasing the apartment. As a matter of fact, it motivated me to find a solution for the same situation. Where there is a will, there is a way.

In any problem you face, there is always a solution; it all depends on how much you are willing to give in order to reach the solution. You must give something extra into your investments in order to get the best out of it. You must give something to get something.

Finding Financial Independence

When I was still playing football, I learnt that the difference between a star and any other player, is that the star was willing to give much more into the training than the other players were willing to give. That way the star harnessed the best of himself. The difference between the player I was before Swaggy and the player I was after Swaggy, was that when Swaggy came, I pushed myself the extra mile in order to be a sought after and well-paid footballer.

I therefore found a solution for the issue. I decided to spend a little extra money to install security and monitoring systems in order to prevent losses. That way my profits will not leak; they will grow fast enough to repay the extra I spent on security, and will continue to flow in. I installed a camera at the door; a wireless camera with a motion sensor. This way, I could always get an email notification showing me a photo of who was entering my apartment. I also changed the property management; I did not use the same property management because they were already used to their way of doing things; they would not change their ways. It was better to train new management with fresh minds. I wanted to manage it myself, but I lacked experience. I was, however, a quick learner and my experience with working as an Accountant came in handy. I was able to be hands-on with the apartment, and I was able to reconcile all accounts. This prevented any shady deals by the new management.

Chapter 9
The Joys of Passive Income

We finally got the apartment in March 2019, and in a couple of days of listing it on Airbnb, we got our first bookings. We were excited. A couple of hours after our first booking, another booking came in and the bookings just kept rolling in. We were always 85-90% booked from both Airbnb online platform and walk-in guests. I gave the staff an incentive that if they got me guests, I would pay them some money on a per guest basis. The staff helped, but I must say 70% of my guest came from Airbnb. Our resort apartment ended up being the best investment we could have made. I told Swaggy, my Jesus never fails. He always sees the end from the beginning and He sometimes uses our adversity to get us to our destiny. If we did not have the issue with my football team, we would never have been here on time to purchase this apartment. God always has a plan for our good, even in the midst of our troubles.

We are now financially independent. We can cater for all our expenses and still have an emergency fund. Even though we are not rich, we don't have to worry about money or about putting food on the table or paying our bills. One of the advantages of owning a beach front apartment in the best location in Jamaica is that we could always go there ourselves and enjoy the best of what Jamaica has to offer, without much expense. It felt great taking my kids there. I felt proud seeing how they were happy; and I kept imagining how one day I could hand over the property to them and tell them, "This is for you."

The feeling we got from making our money work for us was addictive, so much that I started to read and learn about all sorts of passive income. While I was in Vietnam, I was also thinking about investing in the stock market. During my days of working as an Accounting Clerk, one of my aunts used to always tell me, "Junior, you need to invest in stocks and not your savings account." She used to tell me about Barita, but I was too young and care-free back then to take it seriously. My mind was not where it should have been. However, getting married and having kids changed my mindset. I chose to learn about stocks.

In the process of learning about stocks, I attempted to invest. However, I was set on investing on the New York Stock Exchange; I wanted to be the next Warren Buffet. I was brought to my low when I came to learn that I could not do so without a social security number. One day, while reading the news, I saw an article on the Bloomberg Business with the headline, "It's Jammin':

Jamaica's Tiny Stock Market Conquers World in 2015." The news article explained that the Jamaica Stock Exchange (JSE) was the best performing stock exchange in 2015. Jamaica was the best again in 2018 and had been in the top 5 by 2019. Imagine how shocked I was. Here I was looking to invest in America, when I was actually sitting on the best market in the world. That was when I started to recount what my aunt was telling me about Barita Investment Limited. I immediately called Barita to set up an appointment and get an account open. I had no real experience in stocks, so when I was told to open an account, I needed at least 100 shares in any one company. I picked the best long-term growth companies I could think of in Jamaica; companies which I knew from childhood and that I knew Jamaica could not do without; Grace Kennedy, LascoM, NCB, Wisynco, just to name a few. I bought into those companies in early 2019 and, maybe it was beginners' luck, I was able to sell my shares in LascoM and Wisynco for double the money I invested. Beside this, I was receiving dividend cheques from all the above companies. Now, if it is your first time hearing of dividends, it means when the company makes profits, part of the profit is paid to the owners (shareholders of the company) regularly, after an agreed period.

This is how I became a part-owner of some of the best companies in Jamaica. To give you a clear example, when I bought NCB shares, I bought them at JM$144 per share in 2019. Within a couple of months' time, that same NCB stock moved to JM$250 per share. I felt like 2019 was my year because every stock I bought did great. I was now motivated to become an investor on a bigger level. I started to follow the market more, and to learn more about stocks investment. Investing on stocks and real estate became my bread and butter. I was now staying home with my family every day and still making money. I was no longer thinking about getting a job or going back to school. Don't get me wrong, I have nothing against the two as most people need to start from a 9-5 job before they become investors but, like I have told my sister, even though you are working a 9-5 job, use your 6-10 to build your own dream. Even if you do not have capital for it yet, read something about it to expand your knowledge of it. It will open up your mind, and when opportunity comes, you will spot it easily through any adversity, and it will find you prepared.

I have brought my baby sister, Jody, into my world of passive income. Jody has a masters degree and has always been the most educated of us both, and I am the proudest big brother in the world. Jody has a stable job and is independent. However, at the end of the day, I am her elder brother and I felt it was my duty to get her to own a stock account.

Chapter 10
Riding With Opportunity

Jody became my first student in the stock market. By that time, a new stock was coming on the market by the name of Wigton Farm Limited. Wigton Farm is an energy company that provided 30% of its energy to JPS. JPS is Jamaica's only electricity provider. Wigton was government-owned but was now going to be public. This meant that every single Jamaican could buy a share in the company. What was also great was that it was being sold at 0.50 JMD per share. Compared to the stocks that I bought, which were already listed and established, Wigton was what Americans would call 'a penny stock.' I think the whole country or people who loved to invest in the stock market in Jamaica were excited. There was a great buzz around Wigton; this was going to be my first big investment and it would be my sister's first investment. I was a bit nervous; I was aware that, while it can be very exciting when everything is working and going well, everything is a risk, and stock prices can go up as easily as they can come down. With that in mind, Jody and I bought into Wigton farm.

On June 2019, it was listed on the (JSE) Jamaica Stock Exchange for 0.50JMD per share. By September 2019, it was at US$1 per share. Jody called me with so much excitement in her voice. She had tasted the feeling of letting your money work for you. I was not excited about the doubling of our investment as much as I was excited about sharing this good move with my sister; the feeling of sharing a life-changing concept. I did not give her money, but I gave her something better; I taught her how to let her money work for her and that is what I want to give to everyone and anyone who cares to listen to me.

Chapter 11
Giving Back to My Roots

In 2019, my business life was only about two things: real estate or stocks. Every book I was reading that year was either about real estate or stocks. I was driving around Jamaica looking at developments. I wanted to invest more in both markets. I was bent on giving back as much as I was learning. Growing up in Jamaica, I had never learned about Stock or Real Estate in School, and it really puzzled me. I felt the need to visit my high school, Greater Portmore High School, to speak about my life-changing ventures. I could have gone to many other schools to speak. I had friends who asked me to go to speak in some of the elite schools in Jamaica, because of my achievements as a football player representing Jamaica. I saw this as an opportunity to speak to youth about getting wealthy. I could get through to the boys even more easily than their teachers could do it, because I was not super educated on a book level. I sounded like them, therefore, they felt that I could relate better to them. I was just like them when you think about it; I was the boy who Jamaica did not pay much attention to, until I excelled. You know, I used to ask myself, "If we want a better Jamaica, and we know the schools that the society label as less educated, hard headed, trouble makers, whatever negative label; then why aren't the better teachers sent to those schools to get those kids to catch up with the elite schools?" Instead, sadly, it is the other way around. The best teachers are sent to elite schools while the lower standard schools are the ones who need them most. This motivated me to reach out to the schools that I came from and try to bridge the gap.

I went to my former school one day. I was invited on career day. I did not plan a speech; I just went and spoke from my heart. I saw the same teachers that were there when I was at school. When the kids saw and heard this, they felt we could identify with each other. They felt we were connected even more because I sat on the same chairs and was taught by the same teacher. They found hope because they saw what I had become, despite going through the same circumstances they were going through.

While I was talking to them about passive income, a teacher asked me what it was. The fact that it was a teacher asking me this question got me thinking hard about our Jamaican education system. I realised that I must not rely on the school system to educate my child about building wealth. I had nothing against the school, I simply realised that the responsibility of teaching our children about building wealth lies with the parents. I was given one hour to speak to the kids, but at the end of the hour, the kids did not want to leave the room. They were hungry for this new thing they were learning; it was something real; something they had never heard before; it gave them motivation. They were asking many questions such as: "What is a stock? What are shares? How do I buy them? Why isn't my home really an asset?" The questions kept coming and I found myself smiling. I remember saying to myself, "I found my purpose." I wasn't being paid anything to speak to the children, but I was receiving something money could not buy: the joy of changing lives and my country. I was so motivated.

I took my camera a few days later, went by Ascot High School, which was close to my home, and interviewed the kids before they went to school, just to shine light on the things I thought they should know and to spark a thought process within them. This gave me a lot of satisfaction.

Chapter 12
Spin Many Wheels

The books I was reading were teaching me that the wealthy people did not have one stream of income, they had multiple. Here I was finding myself slowly creating those same things. I had our beach front apartment on Airbnb; I had stocks paying dividend, and our latest addition would be our YouTube channel. We were making money in our sleep and in ways which we did not have to trade too much of our time for money. All that our passive businesses needed was a small amount of our time and, in return, they gave us more time to live life on our terms.

The thing about building wealth is that it is a very slow process and requires patience. While speaking with subscribers who wanted to also buy beach front properties like me, I could identify with their excitement, but I taught them that patience was really important. The thing with real estate is that it can be very difficult to sell property, if it is not in the right location. What I learnt from owning property at Fisherman's Point is that location is the key to having a good cash flow in the Airbnb business. There were many properties for sale in that area, and many interested investors may have assumed that if they bought any, they would automatically find the same success I did in Airbnb. This was far from the truth. After speaking to many tourists who came many times to Ocho Rios, I noticed one thing; if they came the first time and booked on the hills because they did not know about the apartments close to the beach, then on the trips that followed, they would make sure that they always booked the apartments by the beach. They expressed that after soaking up the sun and swimming, one would want their beds and shower to be seconds away and that is what Fisherman's Point gives them.

What I realized, while checking the calendars of Airbnbs that were far away from the beach, was that they were always empty. They were only booked after the ones close to the beach were full. The thing about Ocho Rios Bay beach is that there are limited rooms by the beach, because there are only three villas\apartments by the beach, and a lot of these apartments are owed by senior citizens who bought these apartments as retirement homes. What a way to retire! I can picture myself and Swaggy doing that in a couple of decades.

I want my patreons and subscribers to understand that it is better to wait to buy in the right location, than to get excited and buy into something that was readily available but not at a good location. I have the experience to back it up and you can trust me.

Chapter 13

Diamonds in the Dirt

A wealthy mind sees the diamonds in the dirt. When I say a wealthy mind, I am not just talking about rich people; I am talking about a mind that can see opportunities in the midst of problems. It is this kind of mind that attracts wealth.

There is always something good in what you despise. Stories are told around the world of people or communities who despised their barren and arid land and sold it cheaply to wealth-minded people who explored it and found great treasure in it. When others see nothing but dirt, a wealthy mind sees the diamonds beneath the dirt.

I do not want financial freedom just for myself; I want it for every Jamaican. I know we have many challenges, but I see potential for Jamaica to be one of the most respected economies in the world. We have the resources we need; what we need to do is educate and change hopeless minds into wealthy minds, one mind at a time.

I feel restless about how Jamaica is being bought up by everyone but Jamaicans. Foreigners see the potential and the value of Jamaica more than us. Jamaica has the perfect location. Look at the potential for the shipping industries. Jamaica is an English-speaking country; look at all the natural resources that are here.

Let us consider Harlem in the USA. When I was growing up, I saw Harlem as a hotspot for drugs and crime. I remember being in New York in 2016; I had taken Swaggy and Lionel on a trip to Times Square. We visited the famous Manhattan with families I had been staying with in the Bronx. While we were walking and looking at the beauty of Manhattan, my cousin asked, "Do you know where we are now?"

I said "No."

He said, "This is Harlem." I was shocked. He said, "A couple of decades ago, you would think twice before walking here; look at it now!"

I saw so many different races. Back in the days, whites and other races would not set foot in Harlem. The area looked well developed. That was what gentrification does. My cousin said the natives of Harlem did not see the potential of what they had, therefore, most of them abandoned or sold their property. Most people did not even own where they lived, therefore, the cost of living eventually pushed them out. I felt fearful that maybe one day, that would happen to Jamaica.

Do you think the gentrification of Jamaica is possible? Do you think we can have a Jamaica without a thousand people dying per year? A Jamaica without corruption in its government? While it seems hard to believe, I do not think it is impossible, and I do believe that change is coming; slowly, but it is coming. We only need to give something in order to get something out of our beautiful country.

We can change this country by owning a piece of it at a time, and by educating the youth to do the same. I often wondered if I was somehow lucky or my situation was different because I was a football player. There are moments of discouragement when my mind was filled with doubts about my mission.

While the devil was trying to steal my mission, I ran into a young man by the name of Miguel. He was from the UK. He was born there to Jamaican parents and only knew Jamaica by way of decent. While in UK, Miguel fell on hard times and was advised by family members to take a trip to Jamaica. Miguel had been buying properties in UK and had a deal go bad. While relaxing in Jamaica, he saw some apartments by the beach; this was in 2014. Just like me, Miguel bought one. He was also surprised at its earning potential, so much that he mortgaged three more. Miguel now has four apartments and a home in Jamaica.

I want you to always remember this; after every storm there is calm and a ray of sun. Little did Miguel know that his bad deal in the UK would be the blessing he needed for his success in Jamaica.

You see, Miguel was not a pro soccer player. He was a regular guy who had a dream to be a boxer. However, he had to focus on being a realtor who ended up back where his parents started. Miguel's story came at the right point in time, as sometimes the motivator himself needs motivating. His story motivated me once more to carry on with my mission of changing our nation, one mind at a time. I was now fully able to say from my heart that anyone can make it. Even if you are working a 9-5 job, you can still make it work for you. Ask yourself, "What is the best form of pension you could work towards?" Get your hands dirty; increase your effort and work smart towards ownership. For example, you can buy a property by the beach that would appreciate over time, pay for itself and also bring in added income.

Chapter 14
Riches Are For Positive Minds

What I want you to take from this book is that it does not matter where you begin. As long as you have vision and you keep your focus, you too will own your property and will have money working for you. You can be financially independent, regardless of your current situation.

Everything I learnt about stocks and real estate was self-taught; I did not learn it in school, neither did I learn it from my parents. It is time for us to take control of our lives and our time. I now consider myself to be financially educated, and I hope this book, which is the first in a series of books, will plant seeds of wealth in your mind and life that will help you find financial independence.

I want to introduce you to a term I learnt about: FIRE. It stands for **Financial Independence Retire Early**. It is a movement geared towards financial independence. The movement, FIRE, is known for its extreme savings and investing. In my younger years of adversity, I was making my way to FIRE without even realizing it. I have had countless patreons on my Patreon account asking me what is my FIRE number, meaning, what does it take for you to survive monthly in Jamaica. I challenge you to find your FIRE number. In order to retire early, you must know what your expenses look like. As for me, I had to write down on a piece of paper my water bills, electricity bills, mortgage, salary for housekeeper for our Airbnb, and the same expenses for our home, including school fees for the kids and any other miscellaneous expenses. We found a total number of all our expenses per month, and we needed our real estate investing and stock investments to cover all our expenses, plus give us some savings in the form of an emergency fund: this was our goal. We are proud to have been able to reach our goal of financial independence by the grace of God which guides us along this journey. I must emphasize the word JOURNEY, because while we celebrate this small success in life, we realise that the success, in itself, is part of a bigger journey. That is the way I look at it; there is no finish line to success. Today you may be up and tomorrow you may be down, which is why I always keep my heart in humility. I know it only takes one unplanned crisis, such as COVID-19, to render millions jobless and businesses destroyed. I never saw this coming. While writing this book, I am still feeling the effects of COVID-19. However, I continue to soldier on in success' journey.

I believe, beneath the barren dirt, lies diamonds. This adversity will birth great methods of doing business.

Do not look at your failures with regret; be proud that you tried and failed, because it is from failure that great lessons come, and great ideas are birthed. From COVID-19 came this book which will change many lives for better in Jamaica and beyond; a legacy for my kids and grandkids to be proud of and to learn from. This book will long outlive our family and will become a foundation upon which generations of the Stevens family build upon. Just thinking of this makes me proud.

Final Word

I pass my sincere gratitude to our supportive patreons and over 22,000 subscribers (still counting) on our YouTube channel: "Life with the Stevens." This book was inspired by you. We have received so much love and support, and writing this book, I must say, could not have been possible without you. I spend hours a day trying to respond to every comment on YouTube; to give a helping hand to a brother or sister who wants to start their financial journey.

In writing this book, I hope I will be able to reach every youth in Jamaica. If I change one life, or inspire one, then that gives me great joy.

Our next book should be about the importance of marriage in building wealth. As a man who was not raised in a stable family environment, as many Jamaicans kids can attest to, I have grown in knowledge and experience to see how important it is to raise kids in a stable family environment, and how difficult it is to raise kids, but let me leave that for Book II.

Talk soon.